The New Manager's Handbook

"Now you've earned your reward: a staff to manage. From now on, your success no longer depends on just your technical abilities and specialized knowledge. You will only prosper if other people do their jobs well."

"Managing people can be an experience that makes you feel really good about yourself—as long as you understand that it's not a tidy, orderly, predictable business. Flexibility and maturity will come in handy. So does a dose of good-natured humor that brightens everyone's day."

"Your job as a manager isn't to teach employees everything they need to know, but to let them learn on their own. Then you wind up with a more motivated and intelligent team."

The New Manager's Handbook

✔ *24 Lessons for Mastering Your New Role*

MOREY STETTNER

McGRAW-HILL

New York Chicago San Francisco Lisbon
London Madrid Mexico City Milan New Delhi
San Juan Seoul Singapore Sydney Toronto

4 5 6 7 8 9 0 DOC/DOC 0 9 8

ISBN 0-07-146332-1

Contents

The New Manager's Handbook

☑ The New Manager

Congratulations on joining the ranks of management. Your hard work has paid off, and now you have responsibility for supervising the work of others to help your organization achieve its goals. While your expertise and success in your work has likely contributed to your promotion to manager, you're probably aware that this new position requires a different set of skills—skills that require effective interaction with other people at work. These people include those you supervise, your peers, and the managers you report to.

There's an old joke that disgruntled employees sometimes tell each other. "You know the definition of manager, don't you?" "No, tell me." "A manager is the person who sees the visitors so everyone else can get the work done." Maybe that's funny to some people, but now that you're a manager, it's your job to laugh *with* your staff, rather than having them laugh *at* you.

This book is designed to help make sure that happens and to help you make the transition effectively. It will provide you with a quick guide that you can refer to as you figure out how to execute your new responsibilities.

At the heart of managing are planning and communication, and you'll find numerous lessons hear the deal with the nuances of these skills, including giving feedback to your employees to help them improve their performance and keep up the motivation, how to give great instructions to get the results you're looking for, how to build alliances, and how to listen to others. You need to learn to run meetings that employees know will help them successfully work together; you need to learn how to think strategically as well as tactically; you need to learn how to build alliances. And while you may understand the theory of these things, it's actually doing them that is the issue. And that's also the point of this little book—to give you practical methods for meeting the challenges of managing your employees and making the organization happy it has you doing this work.

It's a good idea to first read this book from beginning to end. Highlight ideas that intrigue you. Make notes in the margins. Think about how you can use the methods to help you as you immerse yourself in your new responsibilities. Then keep it in your office as a quick reference. Build on the ideas and actions described here to hone your management skills. Soon enough, you will no longer be a new manager, but one who clearly understands the nature of your responsibilities and the opportunities you have to make a real difference for your organization and yourself. Good luck!

"In the end, all management can be reduced to three words: people, product, and profits. People come first."

—Lee Iacocca

☐ ~~Give criticism~~

☑ Give feedback

Part of your job as a new manager is to give help-ful feedback to employees. But it doesn't stop there.

The feedback process isn't over when you reel off what you think the employee should do to improve performance. It ends when the worker understands your input and applies it successfully.

Most managers dislike giving negative feedback. They may fear that workers will perceive their well-intentioned comments as personal criticism. And because it's common for rookie managers to want to be liked by their troops, they may shy away from pointing out work-related defects or concerns about an individual's effort or attitude.

Get over it!

Effective managers must give feedback every day. It can range from glowing praise to neutral observa-tion to serious alarm. Ideally, positive input should far outweigh everything else. Employees crave com-pliments from their supervisor—they remember them, treasure them and share them with friends and family.

Look for opportunities to point out what workers are doing right. Don't feel you must ration praise only for rare flashes of brilliance or exceptional results. Letting people know that you admire how they handle a customer, organize their workspace or analyze a problem is in itself a form of feedback that strengthens your relationship with your team.

When your goal is to provide constructive feedback that helps employees improve, set the stage. Get a two-way conversation going. Discuss the high standards you set for yourself and your crew—and find out what the worker thinks of these standards. That's better than coming right out and saying, "Here's something you're doing wrong that you need to work on..."

Remember that almost all workers thirst for input. One of the employees' biggest complaints is "I don't get enough feedback from my boss." Remove the mystery. Freely share your ideas, suggestions and reservations. Make individuals aware of their performance and guide them to improve.

Use this three-step method to deliver feedback that sinks in:

Invite employees to evaluate their performance: Let them rate a specific aspect of their work based on, say, a 1-to-10 scale or an A-to-F letter grade. Many people judge themselves more harshly than you would. Even if they inflate their rating, it gives you a baseline to respond with your input.

Ask follow-up questions: Dig for more information. Get employees to share details or examples that justify their self-rating. Notice what criteria they use to evaluate themselves and how they track their performance.

Align your analysis with their comments: Now that you've given employees a chance to chime in, it's your turn. Begin by thanking them for explaining how they view their performance. Then add, "I'd like to piggyback on what you've said." Start by giving feedback that they missed. Then endorse positive input that you heard earlier (as long as you agree) and add some fresh praise so you end on a high note.

"The good ones among managers ... do not talk to their subordinates about their problems, but they know how to make the subordinates talk about theirs.

—Peter Drucker

☐ Cover up bad news

☑ Make the best of bad news

The way you express bad news will make or break your credibility as a manager. If you level with employees, you show that you're a no-nonsense leader who prizes clear communication. But if you talk around the issue, others may follow your example and avoid addressing problems that need attention.

Prepare to deliver bad news. Decide in advance what you want to accomplish by speaking up. Do you want to spur your employees to take action or simply raise their awareness? Is there an upside to the situation and, if so, should you emphasize it? Do you want to discuss the evolution of the problem or limit your comments to the here-and-now?

Maintain your perspective. New managers sometimes blow bad news out of proportion by "awfulizing" it to the point where it takes on a life all its own. Realize that setbacks come with the territory;

take them in stride and convey bad news to others so they, too, see the situation accurately rather than as Armageddon.

Watch your tone and mannerisms. Speak in succinct, straightforward terms. Give the facts without editorializing. For example, skip phrases such as "I hate to tell you this" or "This is the part of my job I dread most" and jump right to the point.

Don't sigh, shrug and repeatedly shake your head in dismay. Imagine you're Walter Cronkite reporting the news with an undercurrent of strength and perseverance in your voice. If you start flinching or feeling too overwrought about it, your employees may focus more on your pained demeanor than the news itself.

End on an upbeat note. Set a goal for future improvement or present a strategy that addresses the source of the problem. Left to fester, bad news can hurt morale. Dangle hope or offer solutions to boost employees' attitudes.

Here are three techniques to make bad news more palatable:

Display "ego strength": Show that your ego isn't threatened by the bad news. Use non-defensive language such as, "I take responsibility for contributing to this state of affairs, and I take responsibility for leading us out of this." As a new manager, you can say, "I'm learning every day, so I want you to know what I've learned."

Set the context: Tie a specific piece of bad news to larger organizational goals. Say, "This adds to our challenge, but we can overcome it."

Get to the point: Stay on track and don't waste words. State the most important news up front. Then add facts, evidence or other supporting information.

"Communicate everything you possibly can to your partners. The more they understand, the more they'll care. Once they care, there's no stopping them."

—Sam Walton

☐ Do it all yourself

☑ Delegate

Effective managers must have faith—in their people. Your success depends on your willingness to rely on employees to take initiative, solve problems, and produce results.

You've surely heard the advice: delegate when possible. But it's not that simple. If you do it the wrong way, delegation can backfire.

Andrew Carnegie said, "The secret of success is not in doing your own work but in recognizing the right man to do it." Delegation thus takes forethought. Match the right employee with a challenging assignment.

Consider an individual's *interests*, *strengths*, and *expertise*—and hand off tasks to employees who rate highly in at least two of those three categories. If you want someone to research and respond to customer complaints, for instance, delegate the project to an employee who enjoys serving customers, possesses excellent people skills, and knows how to investigate problems and dig for answers.

By delegating, you improve your efficiency. You can focus on high-priority issues and not get bogged down in work that depletes your time and energy. At the same time, you can develop your employees and make them more valuable contributors.

Don't confuse delegation with assigning routine work to employees that falls within their normal job duties. True delegation involves giving someone the responsibility and authority to do something that's normally part of *your* job.

Delegation is not "dumping." If employees think you're tossing the least desirable assignments on their lap, they'll resent it.

Set up controls and checkpoints to monitor your employees' progress. Discuss how you can both evaluate progress and measure a project's success.

Define clear goals and expectations for the assignment. But don't explain how to do it. Let others discover for themselves how to follow through.

New managers often assume that once they delegate, they're no longer accountable for the results. But handing over responsibility and authority to employees has its limits. Ultimate accountability remains with you—whether you realize it or not.

Rookie managers sometimes fall into the trap of taking an assignment back unwittingly. They might say, "Here, let me show you," and they wind up doing the whole project. Avoid this by letting employees problem-solve for themselves.

Follow these pointers to delegate well:

Step back: Select tasks that employees can control and implement on their own. Make sure the individual can exercise judgment and autonomy. If you micromanage, delegating does more harm than good.

Clarify the assignment: Confirm that employees understand the purpose, the goal and the performance measures you'll use to judge success. Remove ambiguities and set a clear deadline.

Run an "I'm not here" test: Identify key aspects of your job—and decide who could handle those responsibilities in your absence. By anticipating what you want employees to do when you're not there, you can delegate pieces of your managerial duties to them now so they're ready to step in later.

"Strange as it sounds, great leaders gain authority by giving it away."
—James B. Stockdale

☐ Departing workers have nothing to say

☑ Pick the brains of departing workers

When an employee quits, you have a golden opportunity to learn how to do your job better. How? On or just before the worker's last day, schedule an exit interview.

People on the way out the door often speak freely about how they—and their co-workers—view management. All you have to do is ask smart questions and listen.

Invite departing employees to give their opinions about what you and your organization do right and wrong. Take notes. Show interest in their observations and follow up.

Most employees, even embittered ones, will remain civil while sharing information and insights that make you a stronger, wiser manager. Once they

17

see you're eager to pick their brains, they'll usually open up.

Don't assume departing employees will use the exit interview to settle scores with colleagues, unleash their pent-up anger at company policies or lecture you about misguided change campaigns, or management screw-ups. Asking neutral questions helps. "Can you describe the level of teamwork you've experienced?" is better than "Are you disappointed in our teamwork?"

Assure employees of confidentiality. Explain that you value their input and you want them to raise honest concerns.

Exit interviews can help you identify reasons for high turnover or poor morale, expose poor working conditions, and gain ideas that sharpen how you manage. Longtime workers can reflect on their years at your organization, pointing out pros and cons of various policies, procedures, or personnel. They may know what works and what doesn't—and who are the unsung heroes in your unit. An exit interview is one of the only ways for new managers to gather such valuable insight.

Better yet, your genuine interest in the departing employee's views can leave a lasting positive impression. The individual may come away feeling better about you, and this can work in your favor later. Cultivating allies outside your organization helps you build a valuable network.

To squeeze the most knowledge from departing workers:

Lay the groundwork: Let employees know in advance what you're going to ask. Emphasize that you treat their opinions seriously and you hope they'll give considerable thought to the issues before the interview.

Separate tangibles from intangibles: Ask two sets of questions. First, focus on fact-finding (example: "Did you have the tools and resources you needed to do the job?"). Then shift to less concrete, hard-to-measure areas such as morale and camaraderie (example: "How would you rate the work ethic of your team?").

Request names: Collect referrals for new hires, vendors, and consultants. Probe to find the names of the individuals your departing employees respect most both inside *and outside* your organization. Discuss your hiring needs and invite the employee to stay in touch and refer top candidates to you in the weeks and months ahead.

"Most of the successful people I've known are the ones who do more listening than talking."
—Bernard Baruch

☐ ~~Review performance once a year~~

☑ Review performance regularly

Most employees hunger for information on how they're doing. They want a boss who administers regular performance reviews—and provides a thorough, thoughtful evaluation that's constructive and well supported.

Many new managers dread performance appraisals, especially when meeting with employees with poor or inconsistent performance. What's worse, the review process in many organizations is a burdensome administrative task that requires reams of paperwork.

Formal performance reviews become easier if you informally update employees about the quality of their work throughout the year. If they know on any given day what they do well and what they need to improve, then there will be few surprises during your regularly scheduled appraisals.

Balance strengths and weaknesses when reviewing someone's performance. Don't go overboard in either direction. If you dwell on employees' defects, you may overlook what they do well and deaden their spirit. But nonstop gushing can lead workers to conclude they can do no wrong in your eyes. Aim for at least a 3-to-1 ratio of pointing out what's right and what's wrong about an individual's performance.

Stick to the facts. Describe performance based on what you've seen firsthand or solid evidence you've collected. Give dates and times to substantiate your observations. Avoid labels like "careless" or "sloppy." Instead, cite concrete reasons *why* you perceive someone this way. One of the hardest lessons for new managers to learn when reviewing employees' performance is to allow the workers to judge for themselves how they're doing—after citing specific examples of their actions.

Strive for accuracy. Unseasoned managers tend to gloss over employees' performance problems by rating individuals as "fine" or "above average" in all categories without much thought. That's risky. If a worker's performance declines to the point where termination becomes an issue, you may lack the documentation you need to prove that person's performance was already shaky at the last performance appraisal.

Here's how to capitalize on performance reviews:

Stick to a schedule: Employees are counting the days until their next review, so honor your commitments. Whether you promise appraisals quarterly, semiannually or annually, follow through. If you postpone reviews or force employees to nag you because you forgot, you'll kill morale.

Use the DISC formula: DISC stands for "describe impact, specify consequences." When you assess performance, describe the specific behavior, discuss its impact, specify what you want to happen and explain the consequences—both good and bad—based on the employee's response.

Suggest, don't threaten: Make sure your goal in reviewing someone's performance is to impart knowledge that allows them to improve. Rather than insist that a receptionist's curt demeanor must stop, focus on how much there is to gain by adopting a more genial manner.

"It's only as we develop others that we permanently succeed."

—Harvey S. Firestone

☐ ~~Make snap decisions~~

☑ Decide and deliver

Now that you're a manager, you'll need to make more decisions than ever before. And you will probably wish you had more time, more information, and more guidance before making tough calls.

By developing a system for calm, rational decision-making, you'll gain confidence when operating under duress. You can decide quickly and deliver great results without backtracking, dallying, or leading others to question your judgment.

Decisions revolve around three steps: gathering facts, identifying options, and choosing the best one. Relevant facts can come from a range of sources, from employees to customers to activity reports and other quantitative measures.

Listing your full range of possible moves requires an open mind. Options that may seem off-the-wall or foolhardy at first may prove worthy of consideration, perhaps when combined with other alternatives. When deciding among all your options, you'll want to apply objective criteria to pinpoint the most sensible, effective choice of action.

Delay can wreak havoc on your decision-making. Waiting induces stress. It prolongs uncertainty and can lead others to doubt your managerial muscle. Collecting facts and weighing options need not be a long, tortuous process.

If you're facing a series of unappealing options, ask yourself, "What's the worst that can happen?" Evaluate the likelihood of different outcomes and isolate variables you can control. This way, you can weigh the worst-case odds against more acceptable outcomes.

Indecision thrives if you're reluctant to accept accountability for your actions. You may not want to provoke others by making a controversial decision or take a stand that turns out wrong. Or you may be overwhelmed by the complexity or magnitude of the decision—and look for excuses to postpone making it.

Combat indecision by setting a deadline. Force yourself to make the best judgment possible with the facts available within a set time frame.

To communicate decisions that might upset others, use diplomatic phrases such as, "I understand your position, but I have to weigh what's best for this organization" or "There are arguments to be made on all sides, so it's particularly tough in this case to please everyone."

To march confidently toward a decision:

Address ambivalence head-on: Acknowledge uncertainty; don't brush it aside. Examine why you're ambivalent. For example, your gut instinct may conflict with what the facts lead you to conclude. Write down your doubts and view them from a detached, dispassionate point of view.

Create a contingency plan: Devise a backup plan in case your decision turns sour. Prepare to mitigate your losses.

Use best- and worst-case scenarios as bookends: Consider the full spectrum of outcomes, from best to worst. Then take steps that minimize the worst case.

"The fact is you'll never have all the information you need to make a decision—if you did, it would be a forgone conclusion, not a decision."
—David Mahoney

☐ Don't worry about praise

☑ Exert "praise motivation"

There's no mystery to motivating employees. It's all about expressing your sincere admiration for them. When they know that you respect their effort, ability, and work product, they're more apt to enjoy their job and heed your directives.

Genuine praise is the ultimate energizer. Think how much more motivated you've become when bosses have applauded your performance. It's a surefire way to build individuals' confidence and push them to excel even more.

The irony is that while most managers know praise serves as a superb motivator, putting that knowledge to work often poses a challenge. Daily pressures, crises, and mishaps may make it hard for you to feel positive about your employees. It's easy to overlook what they're doing right when what goes wrong demands so much of your time and attention.

Praise can take many forms. You can send non-verbal signals such as a pat on the back, an approving nod, or the thumbs-up. Or you can drop quickie comments that make an employee's day such as, "Fine work" or "You outdid yourself this time."

There are more subtle ways to praise. For instance, you can ask employees for their opinions. Preface your question by saying, "I'd like to pick your brain" or "You can probably shed some light on this for me." Don't hint what you want them to say. Just listen, and you'll make them feel important.

Another simple motivator is to use employees' names when you chat with them. You'll get off to a great start as a manager if you learn everyone's name quickly and weave it into conversations. Workers respond more enthusiastically when their supervisors speak to them in a friendly, personal tone.

Rookie managers sometimes assume they should ration their praise. Otherwise, they may figure that employees will come to expect it all the time. Yet there's no such thing as too much praise as long as it's grounded in real accomplishment. Whenever a staffer earns your admiration, say so.

Praise works best when it's specific. Expressing gratitude never hurt, but if you explain *why* you're thanking a worker, you heighten the effect. Get in the habit of saying, "Thank you for ..." rather than just blurting out "Thanks" and moving on.

Better yet, find new ways to communicate your praise. Write a note, send an e-mail card, or give a small gift or half-day off in exchange for exceptional work. The more you can convey your thanks creatively, the more your employees will strive to earn it.

Master "praise motivation" by embracing these work habits:

Catch employees at their best: Look for examples of stellar work. Set high standards and never miss a chance to congratulate someone for exceeding them.

Acknowledge effort, not just results: Some employees will try—and fail. That's the ideal time to say, "I like the way you tried so hard." Don't just shrug and say, "Oh well, at least you tried" or "Maybe next time." Recognize effort as praiseworthy in itself.

Say it once—with feeling: Praise loses its luster if you repeat yourself too often. Find fresh traits, skills or actions to compliment. And once you say it, don't keep restating it until the employee's face lights up. Some individuals don't react to praise with visible delight, but that doesn't mean they disregard it.

"There is no verbal vitamin more potent than praise."

—Frederick B. Harris

☐ ~~Run meetings off the cuff~~

☑ Plan your meetings

In most cases, the best meetings are short meetings.

One of the reasons that meetings get such a bad rap is that they tend to drag on too long. That often happens when a few individuals monopolize the proceedings, or the group constantly veers from the high-priority issues.

New managers who aren't accustomed to running meetings may defer too much to attendees. Or they may overcompensate for their lack of experience by playing the tyrant and stifling healthy debate. By preparing well and keeping everyone focused on what counts, you can save time while building consensus or generating buy-in.

Before the meeting, narrow the scope. Craft an agenda that defines a specific problem and seeks ways the group can address it. Don't overload the meeting with too many disparate issues.

Distribute the agenda in advance, along with related data that you want everyone to absorb ahead of time. That way, you won't waste time in the meeting engaging in information-sharing. Make sure the discussion focuses on solutions, not defining the problem.

Set up the room to advance your agenda. If you want to encourage free-flowing discussion, arrange the chairs in a U or circle. If you're eager to reach fast decisions in an abbreviated meeting, remove the chairs so everyone must stand. Fill out flip charts in advance so you don't bore attendees while you do lots of writing.

To rivet the group's focus on the overriding goal of the meeting, write it down and post it on a side wall. Point to it whenever the discussion threatens to head off course as a silent reminder to everyone to stay on track.

Look at everyone in the room when you speak. Don't just establish eye contact with one or two people or you'll risk excluding others. Notice when someone's trying to get a word in. Recognize quiet or shy individuals, and give them ample opportunity to contribute. Welcome questions, but don't hesitate to say "We can answer that later" if necessary.

To make meetings more effective:

Meet and greet at the door: Shake hands with people as they arrive. That's better than arriving early, planting yourself in a chair, looking down and fiddling with papers as others file in.

Open with an overview: Use the first minute of the meeting to state the purpose of the meeting. Also reveal what attendees will gain by the end. Highlight key agenda items and any planned group activities.

Commit assignments to writing: End the meeting by deciding who will do what—by what date. Misunderstandings will result if you skip this step or assume people know what to do next. Write assignments and send a follow-up memo summarizing everyone's job.

"At Intel, agendas ... include information about the meeting's key topics, who will lead various parts of the discussion, how long each topic of discussion will take, and what outcomes are expected."

—Michelle Neely Martinez

☐ ~~Talk more~~

☑ Listen more

When you're an underling, you wind up listening much of the time while higher-ranking folks do the talking. But now that you're a manager, you may think it's your turn to hold court and make others listen to *you*.

Not so fast.

Listening grows even more important when you're a manager. Your success depends on your ability to capture every nuance of what others say, from employees to colleagues to bosses. Tuning out can prove costly: You might miss critical information, make faulty decisions and draw the wrong conclusions.

You must care about what someone says in order to listen. Indifferent or preoccupied people struggle to pay attention. But interested, open-minded individuals listen because they're eager to hear a speaker's concerns, comments and ideas.

Listening would be easy if everyone entertained us when they spoke. But some people drone on, repeat themselves, or mumble in a barely audible voice. Our minds drift quickly and, soon enough, we're pretending to listen when we're really day-dreaming.

Managers cannot afford to fall into this trap. To absorb what others say, note the types of themes or topics speakers choose to raise. If you're on the phone, write one-word labels that represent each of the caller's main points. This enables you to map out what the speaker covers, which will help you remember.

If your mind tends to wander, focus on the here-and-now. Don't dwell on the past or worry about the future. Banish irrelevant thoughts so that you can clear your head and devote all your energy to the speaker.

Signal to others that you intend to listen. If you have trouble hearing, lean closer or turn off a near-by radio. If you're confused by what you just heard, say so. Don't keep nodding mechanically or you may fall further and further behind in the conversation.

Tame a repetitive motor-mouth by jumping in with phrases such as, "So you want me to…" or "Just to make sure I understand…" If someone's appear-ance, accent or voice tone annoys you, imagine you're reading a transcript of the person's remarks. This will help you understand the message on its own terms.

Sharpen your listening skills by using these techniques:

Distinguish between 911 and 411 topics: Speakers who make what they deem an urgent point crave attention. Recognize the seriousness of their point by listening well. If they seek information, clarify what they need and give it to them.

Listen for understanding, not agreement: Make room for differences in opinion or outlook. Don't shut down mentally because someone disagrees with you.

Think "teach me": Strive to learn at least one fresh fact or insight from every speaker. This will stoke your curiosity.

"One often hears the remark, 'He talks too much,' but when did anyone last hear the criticism, 'He listens too much?'"

—Norman Augustine

☐ ~~React to events~~

☑ Think strategically

The past decade has introduced the term "knowledge worker" to the workplace. That likely makes you a "knowledge manager."

Employees at all levels are expected to *think*—to propose ideas and streamline production or customer service so the organization runs better. As a manager, your role is to devise strategic plans and communicate them dynamically to your team. These plans provide goals and direction for how you and your employees can effectively do your work for the organization.

Thinking strategically is a learned skill. You develop strategic savvy by asking smart questions, digging for answers, and looking past assumptions or "truths" that limit your perspective.

You've probably never given much thought to your strategic thinking prowess. It's not an easy-to-evaluate skill, like typing or writing memos. But now that you're a manager, you must demonstrate your ability to think outside the box and attack challenges with intellectual vigor.

Your bosses will judge you in part on how well you analyze business problems and present creative solutions. They did not climb the ladder by accepting conventional wisdom blindly. By sharing your knowledge and learning from experience, you will impress higher-ups as a strategic whiz.

You need to tap the full range of your intelligence—and the brain power of your staff—to maximize your contribution. Get in the habit of asking penetrating questions of your staff and giving them the time to research the answers. The more you ask, the more you—and they—will learn.

Running a SWOT analysis helps you think strategically (strengths, weaknesses, opportunities and threats). Identifying the pros and cons, along with the opportunities and dangers that might arise, enables you to assess how to proceed. Involve your staff in this exercise. Welcome their input and brainstorm freely. This gives everyone a chance to make each other smarter.

Graduate to a higher level of strategic thinking by applying these tools:

Dig down at least three layers: Look deeper than the surface problem. Keep asking "why." You'll know you've examined an issue in depth when you've dug at least three levels down to expose the inner workings of an issue—the root causes that merit attention.

Perform triage: Separate facts or insights that matter from irrelevant details that you can ignore or file away. Focus only on the most compelling, revealing strands of information to avoid getting buried in a dumping ground of data.

Weigh all sides—and all consequences: Think ahead to identify the repercussions of a strategic decision. Know what's at stake and predict the range of consequences to eliminate nasty surprises later.

"To think strategically is to think with discipline and make informed decisions about the direction you want to go."

—John Woods

☑ Build alliances

You cannot succeed in a vacuum as a manager. You need allies—the more the better.

Yet there's a difference between cultivating friends throughout your organization and being liked by your employees. You should not befriend the people who report to you. Treat them with kindness and respect, but don't expect to socialize with them or confide in them.

Woo allies from among your co-workers and bosses. Seek out folks you admire and get to know them. Exchange favors. Share information. Celebrate joint victories and commiserate over defeats.

Getting people to like you requires tact and sensitivity. For example, while impulsiveness has its place, rushing to say whatever pops into your head almost guarantees that you'll drive away potential allies.

Pause an extra second before you say something even remotely controversial to a colleague. Step into that person's shoes and imagine their reaction. If you're stating an opinion, acknowledge others' views before you volunteer your own. Quote them favorably, praise their actions, and let them know when you've learned from them. As long as you're sincere, you'll attract allies with ease.

Listen for indirect requests for help. If a co-worker mentions that he intends to "read up on the new software," offer to give him a quick lesson. If an executive asks you how she can learn more about a recent shipment of parts, offer to gather all the information she needs and have it on her desk in the morning.

Also pounce on opportunities to solve others' problems. When someone expresses frustration, concern, or uncertainty about a business-related matter, lend an attentive ear. If the person has a big ego, you may want to frame your proposed solutions as questions, not statements. Asking, "Have you tried ..." works better than declaring, "I think you should try ..."

Spread the word when you admire how someone acts. When a colleague wins an award or a senior executive makes a decision you deem gutsy or visionary, tell everyone from your employees to vendors and suppliers. As the messenger of good news, you'll gain allies when the subjects of your admiration hear how much they've impressed you.

Congratulate individuals on their achievements. If a co-worker earns a professional designation or tells you that his son won a college scholarship, offer to host an office party. Your selfless attention to others will not only brighten their day, but it will make your job easier as allies from all sides root for your success.

Follow these steps to gain allies:

Converse, don't compete: Seek to learn from others, not beat them in conversation. Don't try to top their stories or show off your knowledge. Refrain from petty arguments; if you disagree, raise your concerns diplomatically while dignifying opposing views.

Recognize what's right when you hear it: If you like what you hear, say so! At least nod or smile. Keeping a stone face won't endear you to speakers who may wonder if you're listening to them.

Satisfy WIIFM longings: Consider the self-interests of others when you're talking to them. Decide "What's In It For Me" from their point of view—and deliver the goods.

"Getting along with others is the essence of getting ahead, success being linked with cooperation."

—William Feather

☑ Get feedback

Almost all new managers experience bouts of insecurity. They inevitably wonder, "How am I doing? What does the boss think of me? Am I on track to move up—or have I leveled off?"

Few managers get the answers they're looking for.

Despite the popularity of so-called 360 degree feedback—where you receive input from your employees, peers and boss—many managers still wonder how they're perceived. Formalized feedback programs might help you gauge your skills and competencies, but they rarely shed light on your personality traits or the subtle people skills that influence how others respond to you.

Part of the challenge of ascending into management is coping with a lack of feedback, especially from above. Your boss might drop hints (or criticisms) from time to time, but chances are you don't receive ongoing input on certain aspects of your behavior or job performance.

In the absence of feedback, you might grow increasingly uncertain about your abilities. *You* think you're doing a fine job, but without validation from higher-ups your confidence is tested.

You need not accept this sorry state of affairs and remain in the dark about your performance. Choose the right time and the appropriate manner in which to probe for clues. Don't wait for your next performance review in six months or one year, which in itself can prove a letdown. Some executives put off these appraisals or rush through them in a cursory fashion.

Put out feelers so that colleagues and bosses can comfortably report what they think of you. When you turn in work, confirm they received it and ask if it met their needs. After you give a presentation, ask audience members in private if they felt their time was well spent. Follow up after you propose an idea to check whether your co-workers and senior managers approve of it.

Fish for feedback using these methods:

Try indirect queries: If you're on good terms with someone, you can come right out and ask, "Can you give me your honest feedback?" But few people will respond with complete, forthright answers. It's sometimes better to give yourself feedback and see how they react. Example: "I see two areas I need to improve—listening and negotiating contracts. Would you agree?"

Establish a baseline: Once you get to know how someone talks, you can read between the lines when they give you feedback. When someone who prefers words such as "good" or "OK" calls your work "superb," such an uncharacteristically strong endorsement is revealing.

Depersonalize: Rather than ask point-blank for feedback, speak in general terms. Example: "What do you think of people who insist on turning in defect-free work even if it takes them longer?" That's better than saying, "Am I a perfectionist who does good but slow work?"

"Success is all about feedback, feedback, and feedback. You can't run mechanical systems without it, and you can't run organizations without it either."

—Barbara Reinhold

☐ ~~Let them figure it out~~
   ~~alone~~

☑ Give great instructions

One of the biggest traps that managers fall into is they'll fail to communicate exactly what they want—and then they'll get mad when they don't get it.

Now that you're a manager, you'll find yourself giving instructions to employees throughout the day. What you say—and how you say it—will largely determine if they comply.

The task seems simple: Just explain what you want others to do and let them do it. But many obstacles can derail the process. Employees may not listen. You may not speak clearly. Even if they understand perfectly what you want, they may either refuse or otherwise fail to implement it.

You need to strike the right tone when giving instructions. If you over-explain or talk down to workers, they may resent your approach and feel demeaned. But if you bark a series of complex orders, they may wind up confused and unsure where to begin.

Problems can erupt if you rush your explanation or overdose on acronyms or other technical language. Your employees may not know as much about the situation as you do, so you may need to speak in simpler, more straightforward terms. Don't assume they will identify with your ways of thinking.

Customize your instructions to fit the personality and knowledge level of the employee. Consider the person's normal communication style, listening skills, and familiarity with the task at hand. If someone tends to skip ahead and miss key information, for example, you may want to number your steps and ensure the employee takes notes.

The risk increases when you instruct new employees, especially if they're just learning your business. Avoid jargon with new hires. Remove ambiguity from your statements. If any part of your instructions has multiple meanings, the odds of misinterpretation soar. That's when it's particularly crucial to specify how you intend for others to interpret or act on what you're saying.

Focus on action. If you preface your instructions with too much background, you can test listeners' patience. Inserting tangents or giving your opinion as you attempt to give directions will muddy your message. To ensure you deliver your instructions clearly, step into the employee's shoes and make sure you give an instant, one-sentence answer to the question, "What do you want me to do?"

For best results when you give instructions:

Rehearse: Organize your thoughts in advance. Practice on a friend. Confirm that you're able to instruct employees clearly and concisely.

Start simply: Move from the basic to the complex. Give employees a chance to ask questions along the way so they're confident with the fundamentals before having to absorb more complicated stuff.

Ask for a demo: Urge employees to demonstrate their understanding. Don't just ask if they understand; invite them to prove it to you.

"The five steps in teaching an employee new skills are preparation, explanation, showing, observation, and supervision."

—Harold Hook

☐ ~~Speak like a bureaucrat~~

☑ **Speak with power**

As much as former Secretary of State Alexander Haig craved power, he sure didn't talk like a blunt commander. He liked to use phrases such as "caveat my response" and "careful caution." Speaking like a bureaucrat not only undermines your point, but it makes it harder for others to understand and trust you. Set a goal as a manager of becoming a plain-spoken, no-nonsense communicator.

Even if you ascended into management thanks to your technical know-how or your track record of hard work, a good bit of your success now rests on your ability to speak with power. When you talk, you need to ensure others listen.

A mumbling or wishy-washy speaker will prove a dud as a manager. You must state your position clearly and make it hard for others to ignore you. At the same time, you don't want to dominate every conversation.

Strong communication skills revolve around your voice tone, body language, and word choice. By speaking at an appropriate pitch, pace, and volume, you make it easier for people to understand you. By standing tall, gesturing naturally and making friendly eye contact, you radiate poise and leadership. And by choosing vivid words to make your point and limiting your use of qualifiers, you add clarity and force to your remarks.

Powerful speakers hone in on their main point. They chop away fluff and use the fewest words possible to express their core message.

If you see yourself as shy or soft-spoken, that's no excuse to waffle. Giving a half-hearted analysis of all sides or quietly muttering your approval or agreement will not impress your audience. Even if you're bashful or self-effacing, speak in bold, unambiguous terms. Don't drop subtle hints when the situation calls for you to speak up and be specific.

If you want to persuade others, realize that they're more likely to follow you if you're simple and direct. Don't waste words. Beware of giving too much information when trying to explain a point. Filter out extraneous data so that you only talk about what matters most.

Here are three ways to speak with power:

Emphasize action words: Before making an important point, identify the action word in your sentence. Then pause for a half-second or so just before and after you say it. Action drives meaning, so don't rush over your verbs.

Vary your volume: Powerful speakers are not monotones. They whisper to entice others to listen and raise their voice when they're excited or surprised. Keep tweaking the dial on your voice volume to reflect the ebb and flow of conversation.

Paint word pictures: Speak in visual terms to captivate listeners. Rather than tell them what to think, describe what you see in precise, colorful language.

"The finest eloquence is that which gets things done."

—David Lloyd George

☐ Ignore ~~cynics~~

☑ Win over cynics

Ignore cynics at your own peril.

Left unchecked, cynics can drain an organization of its enthusiasm and commitment to excellence. They think they already have all the answers, so they don't listen to reason. Laughing off their sarcastic cracks isn't a long-term solution, because they'll perceive your meek response as a green light to intensify their antics.

One of your toughest tasks as a manager is to shut down cynics and prevent them from infecting morale. It requires constant vigilance.

When employees make caustic comments, challenge them to take a point of view and support it. Don't accept cynical asides if you privately agree or if you're relieved the jab isn't directed at *you*. Respond to all such commentary consistently.

Say that a clerk, Tom, lambastes the "suggestion box" program at your company. Don't nod or roll your eyes as he dismisses the program as a "joke."

Even if you share Tom's disdain for the program, don't say so. Instead, invite him to elaborate. Ask, "What specific steps do you think we can take to improve the program?" Shift the focus from griping to problem solving.

Some cynics need a safe outlet to vent their opinions and observations. You may want to assign a trusted employee to "buddy" with the cynic and serve as a sounding board. Have them meet periodically to share ideas and plan projects. Choose a "buddy" who can withstand cynicism well and who's skilled at redirecting sarcasm into positive action.

By enabling cynics to unleash their stinging jibes in private, they'll be less prone to disrupt staff meetings. Better yet, others will not follow a cynic's lead if they're not exposed to the troublemaker's scathing outbursts.

Rookie managers sometimes stamp someone as a cynic and then disregard that person's views. Ignoring cynics doesn't make them go away.

Also avoid labels. If you view Jim as "Mr. Sarcasm" and refer to him that way behind his back, he may find out, and his attitude might worsen. Nip cynicism in the bud by asking perpetrators to cut back on their biting commentary. Meet with them one-on-one and confront the issue head-on.

To tame cynics:

Remove obstacles so their jobs become easier: If they have a valid point, act on it. Fix a bottleneck in the system that addresses their grievance. Reward their constructive proposals with a quick response to prove that cynicism doesn't pay.

Let critics stage experiments: Empower cynics to take matters into their own hands—within reason. Allow them to make conditional changes as they see fit. Give them limited authority and track the results together. Let them exert power and they'll have less to complain about.

Demand evidence: Cynics tend to make harsh comments without offering support. By asking, "What facts do you have to support that?," you can expose the shaky foundation of their argument. And if they do present a cogent case, help them see how they can enact change by wooing allies rather than adopting an attack mode.

"When it comes to people and their quirks, idiosyncracies, and personality flaws, the variety seems to be limitless. The manager's aim remains the same: to keep these human beings from clogging up the workings of their group."

—Andrew S. Grove

☐ React to change

☑ Prepare for change

Articulate a vision for your employees and you help them appreciate their role in contributing to the organization's success. That's especially important during times of change.

By defining a new direction to move forward, you reassure employees of the benefits of change. You shouldn't have to do this alone. Ideally, your senior management should already know why change will enhance the organization—and give you talking points, which you in turn should pass along to your staff. You can thus become a champion of change by spreading the gospel from above and endorsing it with your own brand of enthusiasm.

If you're left adrift to help your team weather change on its own, don't despair. Identify the advantages of change from your employees' point of view. Appeal to their self-interest and specify what's to gain in both the short- and long-term perspective. If two offices are consolidating into one, for instance, you might alert workers that this will result in better communication with their peers and bosses, better access to technology that makes their jobs easier, and cost savings to the company that will in turn improve their job security.

Beware of sloganeering. Skip the platitudes like "Change is a constant around here" or "We must change or die." Clichés ring hollow with employees. Instead, anticipate their questions and concerns—and be ready to answer them.

If a change may lead to layoffs, relocations or other upheavals that directly affect employees, gather the facts in advance. You may want to develop and distribute a question-and-answer sheet so that employees can read for themselves what's going on and how it will alter their daily routine.

Spend lots of time in informal meetings with your team. The more you can chat face-to-face about the nature of the change and what it'll mean to employees, the more you can dispel rumors and gain their trust about what's in store. Make yourself accessible to everyone.

New managers may not be in the loop about what's going on, so level with workers if you don't have all the answers. Saying, "I don't know but I'll find out and get back to you" works better than barricading yourself in your office and becoming aloof.

Lay the groundwork for change by taking these steps:

Dangle rewards: Explain to the employees what goodies await those who are most adaptable to change. If they can secure a larger office, better equipment or more flexible hours, they might treat change more openly and lower their resistance.

Anticipate multiple outcomes: Employees will want you to tell them the upshot of change: How will things be different? Answer by presenting a range of outcomes and specify what variables will determine how the change will develop.

Withhold negative opinions: Present change in a positive or at least neutral light to employees. Don't dwell on your displeasure with it—or they'll follow your lead and gripe even more.

"Employees don't resist change. They resist being changed."

—Peter Scholtes

☐ ~~Always speak your mind~~

☑ Muzzle your mouth

The most dynamic communicators don't say much.

Instead of trying to talk louder and more force-fully than everyone else in the room, charismatic managers grab everyone's attention by treating their words as a precious resource. They only speak when they have something to say.

Silence enhances your power. By keeping quiet, listening well, and expressing your points in the fewest words possible, you gain a persuasive edge. Your employees will know that every word counts—and they'll give you their undivided attention as a result.

Plagued by nervousness and uncertainty, some new managers talk too much. They'll repeat simple instructions to the point where employees feel insulted. They'll tell long, rambling anecdotes that don't serve a clear purpose to advance the conver-sation. They will interrupt speakers and change the subject. Every time this happens, it threatens to drive away employees who may think, "This person isn't interested in listening to me, so why should I listen to him or her?"

To muzzle your mouth, you need to appreciate the power of silence. That's easier said than done. Many people grow self-conscious during moments of silence in a conversation. Managers may worry that they appear unsure of themselves unless they always have something to say.

By keeping silent, managers often communicate loud and clear. A pregnant pause can convey approval, disapproval, concern, curiosity, or a myriad of other thoughts. It depends on the context of the conversation, your timing, and your facial expression.

Muzzling your mouth works especially well when you want to calm frayed nerves—your own or someone else's! Silence gives everyone a chance to reflect on the situation, rather than inflame it further by making emotionally charged comments.

Another danger of over-talking is that you can bore listeners. Restless employees may no longer heed your directives if you tend to babble. They may start daydreaming the minute you launch into your remarks, thus missing critical pieces of information that you want them to understand.

When you feel the urge to talk, ask yourself if it can wait. Purse your lips shut, breathe evenly and listen.

To tap the power of silence:

Apply the 80/20 rule: In one-on-one conversations, try to listen for 80 percent of the time and limit your speaking to the remaining 20 percent. That requires asking questions to get others to open up.

Stop after you ask a question: When you pose a question, stop. Wait for an answer. If you do not get a prompt response, don't rush to answer your own question or skip it and raise another topic. Waiting in silence for five or 10 seconds may seem like an eternity, but it's sometimes the only way to learn what others think.

Let people vent: When someone's angry or agitated and needs to blow off steam, keep quiet. Saying "Calm down" or "I understand" too often will only make matters worse. (The person may reply, "I *am* calm!" or "No, you *don't* understand!")

"Listen long enough and the person will generally come up with an adequate solution."

—Mary Kay Ash

☐ ~~Ask few questions~~

☑ **Pose penetrating questions**

One of the most overlooked success traits of managers is their ability to ask necessary questions of their employees. Yet the act of asking in itself places you at risk. You may offend or annoy others with your tone or word choice. And you may not like the answer.

Yet questions are irreplaceable tools that enable you to learn. No manager can function well without asking employees lots of questions. By phrasing your inquiries wisely and watching your timing, you increase the odds that workers will level with you.

Employees who have worked for a less inquisitive supervisor may welcome your questions. They may appreciate your willingness to listen and learn, rather than simply tell them what to do. Through your questions, you can uncover ideas and opinions that workers had previously suppressed because no one else had shown interest.

Show interest in each answer. Express thanks when you're given a particularly informative response. Wait an extra few seconds after it appears the speaker's finished before you jump in. This allows others to add more revealing comments that they might otherwise keep to themselves.

Only ask questions if you're genuinely interested in the answer. Staffers can tell in an instant if you don't care about the response. Your distracted air, vacant stare, or flat voice tone may signal that you're going through the motions rather than making a concerted effort to learn. And don't reel off a series of rapid-fire questions or you may lapse into interrogation mode.

Watch your body language as you listen to the response. Remain still and attentive. If you're jittery or your eyes dart around the room, others may sense you're not interested in hearing their answers.

Refrain from excessive nodding and smiling. In your attempt to look supportive, you might go overboard. When you finally tire of sending affirmative signals, the speaker may wonder if you no longer agree or understand what's being said. Also, don't feel you must cluck your tongue or chime in with, "Go on" or "I can imagine" every few seconds, as this can disrupt the speaker's concentration.

Here are some tips to pose penetrating questions:

Keep it simple: Separate statements from questions. Don't lace your inquiries with your observations or opinions. Using the fewest words possible helps you stick to the core question without confusing the issue.

Launch one extra probe: To show you're listening and to confirm you understand the answer, get in the habit of following up when you're discussing an important subject. Use phrases such as, "Just to make sure I got that ..." or "So what you're saying is ...?"

Dig below the surface: Guide employees to think more rigorously. Gently bore into them by asking, "What's the significance of that?" or "What do you conclude from that?"

"My greatest strength as a consultant is to be ignorant and ask a few questions."

—Peter Drucker

☐ ~~Don't give poor performers a chance to improve~~

☑ Lift poor and mediocre performers

Set a high bar. If you accept poor or mediocre performance from your employees, you'll wind up with a bunch of lowly underachievers.

Rookie managers need to push for excellence. Demand the most from people and they'll strive to deliver. Tolerate a halfhearted effort and you send a message that your standards are easy to meet.

By transforming middling workers into high-performance stars, you'll impress your bosses and earn a reputation as a hard-charging, results-oriented leader. Your employees will also feel better about themselves once they see they're part of an elite team. The desire to excel will feed on itself and your staffers will no longer settle for second-rate work.

Accept shoddy performance from others, and it'll bring out the worst in you. Your results may start to slip. Surround yourself with mediocrity, and it becomes harder to give 100 percent. In professional sports, there are many examples of athletes who struggle while playing for a last-place team only to bounce back when they're traded to a playoff contender. The fact that they're suddenly surrounded by a coach and teammates who expect and demand superior performance causes them to dig within themselves and produce better results.

When you spot subpar performance, get involved. New managers may mistakenly spend most of their time with their top employees and avoid everyone else. Ignoring loafers or below-average workers allows them to burrow into your unit. They'll become increasingly difficult to dislodge if you leave them alone.

Chip away at their unacceptable performance by setting incremental goals and cheering their efforts to improve. Reinforce what they do right by praising them. If they lapse into mediocrity, intervene and remind them of your high expectations.

Some workers will resist your entreaties. The more you demand excellence, the more they'll gripe. Don't dignify their complaining by nodding or looking sympathetic. Instead, sever eye contact as soon as they bellyache. This teaches workers that in order to earn your full attention, they must cut the complaints and commit to improving their performance.

To propel poor and mediocre workers to greatness:

Champion their strengths even if they don't: Emphasize what workers do right. Talk up their assets and make them realize how much more they can contribute by harnessing their full potential.

Challenge them to improve in increments: You can't turn slugs into stars overnight. Set short-term goals that require slightly more effort and effectiveness. With each incremental gain, you lift workers onto a higher level.

Enlist peers as mentors: Put your most driven, talented performers alongside your also-rans. Weak employees often respond well when they're influenced by more successful, supportive co-workers.

"We found the most exciting environments, that treated people very well, are also tough as a nail. There is no bureaucratic mumbo-jumbo ... excellent companies provide two things simultaneously: tough environments and very supportive environments."

—Tom Peters

☐ Presentation skills aren't that important

☑ Regale your audience

The ability to deliver a compelling presentation adds a valuable tool to your management arsenal. You'll stand out from the pack by showcasing your charisma and confidence in front of an audience.

The key to win over a small group is to see yourself as a discussion leader rather than a public speaker. Instead of adopting formal mannerisms and recite a prepared speech, you want to spur a dialogue that holds everyone's interest.

Managers are often called upon to speak before an audience. You may need to lead staff meetings, brief senior executives on your unit's progress, or give a presentation at a meeting of your trade group or professional association. Even if you dread the prospect of public speaking, don't shirk from these opportunities. Welcome the chance to learn by doing and refine your skills.

Strive for authenticity when you're speaking. Ideally, you want listeners to come away from your presentation saying, "Now there's someone who's natural on stage!" The more conversational you sound, the more people will pay attention and believe you. If you clear your throat repeatedly, speak in an artificially deep voice or appear wooden instead of animated, you make it harder for the audience to accept you as credible.

Make your first minute count. Begin by grabbing everyone's attention with a captivating observation, a telling anecdote or a startling statistic. Start by talking to the person seated farthest from you. This ensures that your voice envelops the room. If you mutter or mumble in the early going, your audience might decide you have nothing to say and tune out.

Stand up straight. Balance your weight on both feet so you don't lean or slouch. Rest your arms comfortably at your sides and gesture naturally. Just make sure to keep your hands away from your face. You don't want to rub your cheeks, run your hands through your scalp or gesture too wildly so that you wave your hands and arms in front of your face.

Make friendly eye contact with different individuals in your audience. Ideally, look at someone directly while you state two sentences. Then establish a visual connection with a listener in another part of the room for the next few sentences, and so on. Don't let your eyes dart around the room too quickly without locking on an actual person.

Follow these rules to enhance your public speaking:

Customize your remarks: Stay flexible by adhering to a general outline, not a verbatim text. If you read a speech word-for-word, you'll put people to sleep. Invite questions throughout the presentation so you give listeners a chance to chime in.

Engage the whole group: Nervous speakers may focus on two or three allies in the audience and ignore everyone else. Make eye contact with people in all four quadrants of the room. Give equal attention to friends, foes and strangers. Seek out the folks seated in the back so they don't feel excluded.

Use "add-on visuals": Minimize the use of slides. Only incorporate visuals into your presentation if they clearly add something special.

"Presentation: a visual and aural event intended to communicate, for the purposes of providing information, helping to understand, gaining agreement, and/or motivating to act."

—Jennifer Rotondo

☑ Criticize without criticism

As a new manager, there will be times that you'll need to criticize your employees. You'll dread it at first. But with practice it will become easier.

Dishing out criticism tests your communication skills. If you do it right, you can transform it from a negative, stinging message to an empowering, motivating experience for all involved.

Your tone and word choice drive your success. If you sound pained or exasperated, you're already in a hole. Employees will sense your irritation and cringe in despair. And if you're too abrupt, your criticism can come across as hurtful.

Choose words that fairly address the issue at hand. Avoid "always," "never" or "worst," which overstate the case and cause workers to respond defensively.

Also avoid the verbs "is," "was," "has" and "are." These words assign blame—and they equate a person with a faulty characteristic. Example: Replace "Jack is lazy" with "Jack needs to make more calls during the workday." Words work against you when they lead to generalizations or value judgments that grossly exaggerate a performance problem.

Yet words work for you when they describe observable behavior and paint visual pictures of the employee's actions. By saying what you see, your criticism is rooted in solid evidence. And you make it harder for the worker to argue or debate with you.

Before you criticize, ask yourself, "What is the person doing?" Make sure your answer captures exact behavior. If you resort to words such as "slow," "careless" or "unacceptable," you're not reporting actual events; instead, you're judging and labeling someone's behavior.

As a rule, give criticism in private. You don't want to make employees feel self-conscious. Also, begin on a positive note. Use phrases such as, "This may help ..." or "Here's an idea ..." And never criticize an employee's personality; limit your comment to specific actions you want the person to modify or improve.

Speak in a sincere, upbeat manner. If your criticism is well-intentioned, there's no reason to sound hesitant, stern, or downbeat. Your enthusiastic tone will set the stage for the individual's response.

Do not criticize at the same time that you're unleashing pent-up frustration. Managers with fiery tempers should only express criticism when they're calm and in control.

Here's how to give constructive criticism:

Be direct: If you're uncomfortable, you might skirt the issue. But talking around it only prolongs the agony. State your criticism succinctly, free from babbling or dropping hints.

Check your assumptions: Make sure you have faith in the employee to improve. Criticize with the underlying belief that "you're capable of doing better," not "you're a lost cause."

Preserve the employee's self-esteem: Let your employee save face by saying "Maybe you're not aware of this..." or "Here's one suggestion, and I'd like to hear your ideas."

"Never criticize until people are convinced of your unconditional confidence in their abilities."
—John Robinson

☑ Beat the clock

There's no mystery to managing your time. It takes discipline, concentration, and commitment.

New managers may attend time-management seminars and purchase elaborate "efficiency systems" (which usually consist of blank diaries, log books, and daily calendars) under the mistaken impression that they need to load up on fancy tools to succeed.

In fact, all you need is a strong dose of will.

Managing your time requires that you identify your sloppy work habits and fix them. By isolating the wasteful ways in which you plan and perform your job, you can find solutions that enable you to accomplish more in less time.

Rookie managers often struggle with time-management problems relating to procrastination. The new job overwhelms them, and they wind up juggling dozens of priorities at once. They start plenty of projects, but rarely finish them.

To combat procrastination, investigate why you don't want to complete what you start. What's stopping you? Usually, the answer reveals your lack of confidence in the result, your uncertainty over what to do next, or your dislike of the nature of the work itself. To take a common example, new managers who are riddled with self-doubt may fear that by completing a task promptly and turning it in, they'll be vulnerable to criticism and thus prove they're ill-equipped to manage effectively. As a result, they play it safe and stall.

It's normal to worry that you'll be perceived as an impostor posing as a manager. Wave off the anxiety, bear down and deliver the best work you possibly can. Adopting this attitude keeps you on track and enables you to manage your time more productively.

Realize that making a to-do list isn't a solution. It's merely a tool. The endless drafting and redrafting of lists can actually become an impediment that prevents you from taking action. If you're going to list your daily or weekly priorities, keep it simple, and assign a reasonable deadline for each item.

Don't confuse hectic activity with productivity. Immersing yourself in "busy work" might seem satisfying, but you may lose your perspective. Determine what's truly important and shift your attention where it's needed most.

To squeeze the most out of every workday:

Eliminate time-wasters: Identify time killers such as aimless Internet surfing or long, chatty phone calls that divert you from more pressing duties. While it's fine to take short breaks, make sure you *earn* those breaks.

Set realistic standards: Poor time managers tend to be perfectionists. They may dread doing something imperfectly so they refuse to finish it. Strive for excellence, not perfection.

Stage "15-minute bursts": Set a timer for 15 minutes and plunge into a specific task. Even if you don't finish, you'll make headway and generate momentum.

"If you ask [people] what percentage of time they are spending on things that are urgent but not important, most would say 'Half the time.'"

—Stephen Covey

☐ ~~Fear your boss~~

☑ Impress your boss

Just as you manage your employees, you need to manage the boss. Your management career will take off if you can show higher-ups that you're a reliable, trustworthy star.

The very thought of trying to impress the boss may make you cringe. The notion of currying favor with powerful people at your organization may strike you as a fake, calculated attempt to get ahead.

There's a right and wrong way to impress VIPs. If you exceed expectations, anticipate and address a boss's concerns, and consistently look for ways to add value, you'll shine. But if you show off, bad-mouth colleagues, and hog credit for team accomplishments, you'll muddy your reputation and lose any chance of advancement.

Speak in can-do language. Bosses will heed your comments if you sound like you're organized, enthusiastic and eager to deliver results. When they ask you a question, give a one-sentence overview before you dive into the details. For example, start by saying, "We have three options" or "Let's examine this on three different levels."

Look ahead when discussing the status of a project. Focus on what will happen next rather than rehash what's already occurred. And never admit you're in wait-and-see mode. It's better to say, "We're going to make progress when we resume our meeting next week" than "I'm waiting for a return call so we can schedule a meeting next week."

When the boss asks you to do something, respond with confidence. Say, "I'll have that for you by 8:00 tomorrow morning" rather than "I'll try to get that to you tomorrow morning." Don't leave yourself an out. Executives grow suspect of managers who lace their remarks with qualifiers and back off from making bold commitments.

Look for patterns in your interaction with your superiors. Anticipate what issues or requests the boss will raise and be ready to answer. If you promise to do something, follow through promptly. Never make your boss nag you.

Most importantly, adopt a "no excuses" policy. Failing to produce results almost guarantees that a boss will doubt your abilities. When you're asked to give a progress report, start by summarizing what you've done, not what you haven't been able to do. Say, "Here's where we are at" or "So far, we've achieved these five goals." Don't say, "I haven't had a chance to ..." or "I'm hoping that soon I can ..."

Prepare to delight the boss by taking these steps:

Arm yourself with answers: Think in advance of what the boss will ask you—and prepare concise answers. Research the facts and gather the latest information so you're ready to impress with your vast knowledge of an issue.

Underpromise and overdeliver: Set time frames that you can beat. List your project objectives—and then accomplish all of them along with tossing in something extra. Consistently go beyond what's expected and you'll stand out.

Challenge in private: Wait for a calm moment to question a boss's order. Make sure no one else can overhear. Never object to the boss's comments in public.

"Managing one's superior is very similar to that of managing your own customers. In both situations, it simply involves managing human beings and relationships."

—Cynthia Loh

□ Networking isn't important

☑ Mix and mingle

Now that you're a manager, you'll need to upgrade your networking skills. Master the art of small talk, and you can build alliances and develop key contacts both inside and outside your organization.

There's no secret to effective mingling. You simply need to approach strangers at mixers and industry conferences, introduce yourself and ask a friendly question to get the conversation rolling.

Same goes if you're at a company-wide meeting and you don't know the folks sitting next to you. Turn to them and say, "Hi, my name is …" Mention where you work and let the dialogue flow from there.

If you look like you're going through the motions, people will notice. They will detect your lack of enthusiasm or your periodic sighing. Your flat voice tone will convey boredom. And if your eyes wander while someone's speaking to you, it'll appear as if you couldn't care less what they have to say.

Pretending to care when you're distracted or bored will backfire. It's better to muster the energy and curiosity to learn from each encounter, even if you're exhausted or preoccupied.

Think in advance of a few icebreaker questions you can ask. Examples include, "What did you think of the speech?" or "How long have you been participating in this group?" Solicit others' opinions without interrogating them, and they will open up to you.

Follow up on interesting points that speakers make. This proves you want to learn more from them. Don't recite a litany of questions without acknowledging or reacting to the answers.

Look for openings in the conversation to express genuine praise or admiration. If speakers mention accomplishments, such as earning a professional designation or getting a new office or new job title, congratulate them. Prolong their pleasure by asking more questions about their latest triumphs.

When mingling within your company, don't assume your colleagues in other departments (or even your bosses!) know what you're doing. They may not ask what you're working on and how it's going, so you should keep a running list of talking points to weave into the conversation.

To enhance your networking:

Keep it positive: When you meet a stranger, stick to safe, upbeat subjects. Don't complain or talk critically of others.

Restate before you respond: If you need time to mull over an answer or you're uncomfortable with the question, repeat in slightly different words what someone just said. This encourages him or her to elaborate, which in turn helps you buy time to plan the most diplomatic answer.

Know in advance who'll attend: Leave less to chance by reviewing the guest list. That way, you can identify influential people you want to meet and plan how you'll approach them.

"The suggestion to 'network' is nothing more than a fancy way of saying, 'Talk to people.'"
—Peter Vogt

"People are not mathematical equations, so managing them is a fuzzier and more free-form process than inputting hard data."

"Don't believe for a second that just because you're a manager, you're in charge of everything. The fact that you're the boss gives you the right to delegate—to enable others to call the shots on your behalf."

"Employees cannot help but respect a manager who begins by communicating a few core principles—and then exemplifies those principles everyday as everyone works together to achieve goals."

Other Titles in the McGraw-Hill Professional Education Series

The Welch Way: 24 Lessons from the World's Greatest CEO

by Jeffrey A. Krames (0-07-138750-1)

The Lombardi Rules: 26 Lessons from Vince Lombardi—the World's Greatest Coach

by Vince Lombardi, Jr. (0-07-141108-9)

How to Motivate Every Employee: 24 Proven Tactics to Spark Productivity in the Workplace

by Anne Bruce (0-07-141333-2)

The New Manager's Handbook: 24 Lessons for Mastering Your New Role

by Morey Stettner (0-07-141334-0)

The Handbook for Leaders: 24 Lessons for Extraordinary Leadership

by John H. Zenger and Joseph Folkman (0-07-143532-8)

Leadership When the Heat's On: 24 Lessons in High Performance Management

by Danny Cox with John Hoover (0-07-141406-1)

*How to Manage Performance: 24 Lessons for Improving
Performance*

by Robert Bacal (0-07-143531-X)

*Dealing with Difficult People: 24 Lessons for Bringing Out the
Best in Everyone*

by Dr. Rick Brinkman and Dr. Rick Kirschner
(0-07-141641-2)

*How to Be a Great Coach: 24 Lessons for Turning on the
Productivity of Every Employee*

by Marshall J. Cook (0-07-143529-8)

*Making Teams Work: 24 Lessons for Working Together
Successfully*

by Michael Maginn (0-07-143530-1)

*Why Customers Don't Do What You Want Them to Do:
24 Solutions to Overcoming Common Selling Problems*

by Ferdinand Fournies (0-07-141750-8)

*The Sales Success Handbook: 20 Lessons to Open and Close
Sales Now*

by Linda Richardson (0-07-141636-6)

About the Author

Morey Stettner is a writer and communication-skills consultant in Portsmouth, NH. He is the author of the Briefcase Book *Skills for New Managers* (McGraw-Hill, 2000), on which this book is based, as well as *The Art of Winning Conversation* (Prentice-Hall, 1995). A dynamic speaker and seminar leader, he has led hundreds of training programs across the United States on topics such as sales skills, public speaking, and effective listening. He graduated magna cum laude from Brown University.